Careers without College

Physical Therapist Assistant

by Kathryn A. Quinlan

Content Consultant:
Olivia Jean Box
Member, American Physical Therapy Association
Physical Therapist Assistant Program
Jefferson State Community College
Birmingham, Alabama

CAPSTONE
HIGH/LOW BOOKS
an imprint of Capstone Press

CAPSTONE PRESS

818 North Willow Street • Mankato, Minnesota 56001
http://www.capstone-press.com

Library of Congress Cataloging-in-Publication Data
Quinlan, Kathryn A.
    Physical therapist assistant/by Kathryn A. Quinlan.
        p. cm.--(Careers without college)
    Includes bibliographical references and index.
    Summary: Outlines the educational requirements, duties, salary,
employment outlook, and possible future positions of physical therapy assistant.
    ISBN 1-56065-707-3
    1. Physical therapy assistants--Vocational guidance--Juvenile literature.
[1. Physical therapy assistants. 2. Vocational guidance.]
I. Title. II. Series: Careers without college (Mankato, Minn.)
RM705.Q55 1998
615.8'2'023--DC21

                                    97-32102
                                        CIP
                                         AC

Photo credits:
Peter S. Ford, cover, 6
International Stock/Mark Bolster, 19; Frank Grant, 39; Stan Pak, 11, 40, 44;
    Michael Paras, 27
Leslie O'Shaughnessy, 34
Photo Network/Vic Bider, 31; Michael Brohn, 17; Tom McCarthy, 20, 29;
    Mike Moreland, 23
James L. Shaffer, 14, 36
Unicorn Stock Photos/Eric R. Berndt, 24; Tom McCarthy, 4, 12; A. Ramey, 9;
    A. Rodham, 32

Table of Contents

Fast Facts

Career Title _____ Physical Therapist Assistant

Minimum Educational Requirement _____ Graduation from accredited program

Certification Requirement _____ License required in most areas

U.S. Salary Range _____ $20,000 to $48,000

Canadian Salary Range _____ $14,900 to $49,900 (Canadian dollars)

U.S. Job Outlook _____ Much faster than the average

Canadian Job Outlook _____ Much faster than the average

DOT Cluster _____ Professional, technical, and managerial occupations
(Dictionary of Occupational Titles)

DOT Number _____ 076.224-010

GOE Number _____ 10.02.02
(Guide for Occupational Exploration)

NOC _____ 3142
(National Occupational Classification—Canada)

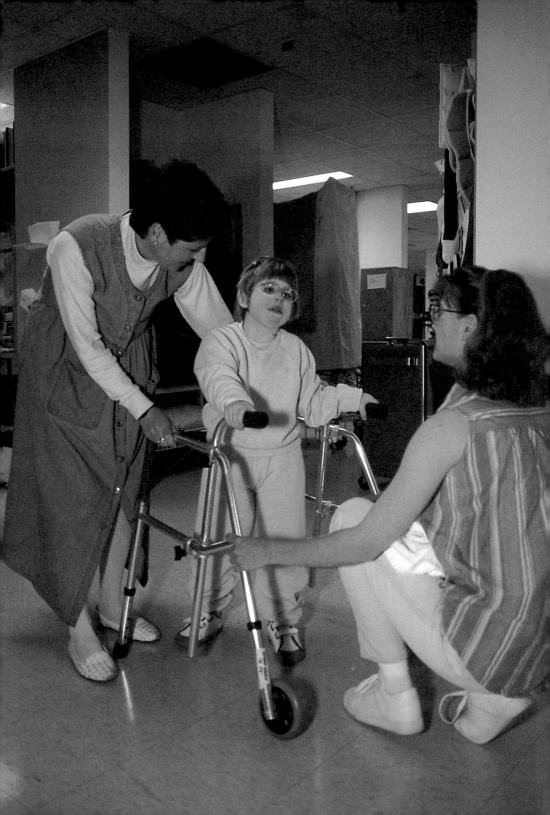

Chapter 1

Job Responsibilities

Physical therapist assistants work with physical therapists. Physical therapy is the treatment of diseased or hurt muscles and joints. Physical therapists use exercise, massage, and heat to treat patients. Massage is the steady pressing and moving of muscles.

Physical therapists work directly with patients. They also consult with doctors on how to treat patients. Physical therapist assistants help physical

Physical therapist assistants help physical therapists with many tasks.

therapists with many tasks. But they cannot work with patients without physical therapists' supervision. Physical therapist assistants are important members of health care teams.

Helping Patients

Physical therapists and their assistants have three main goals. First, they try to help people improve their physical abilities. Second, they try to prevent permanent disabilities and help people get back abilities they have lost. Third, they work with patients to help them feel less pain.

Physical therapist assistants help people of all ages. They treat patients with many different conditions. They help people with severe disabilities. They also help people who have temporary or mild problems. Temporary means lasting for only a short time.

Physical therapist assistants treat people who have arthritis and broken bones. Arthritis is a disease that affects joints. They also help people who have had strokes. A stroke occurs when a blood vessel breaks in the brain. Physical therapist

Physical therapist assistants help people of all ages.

assistants also treat people who were born with birth defects.

Rehabilitation

Physical therapist assistants help patients rehabilitate after an illness or injury. Rehabilitate means to restore to a condition of good health. Physical therapist assistants help patients return to their regular activities as soon as the patients can.

Some physical therapist assistants treat people who have had arms or legs amputated. Amputate means to remove a limb. Doctors amputate arms or legs that are badly injured or diseased. Physical therapist assistants help patients recover after amputations.

Other physical therapist assistants focus on sports injuries. Physical therapy can help athletes recover from injuries more quickly. This allows athletes to return to their sports.

Physical therapist assistants help people improve their physical abilities. They help patients lead active lives.

Physical therapist assistants help people lead active lives.

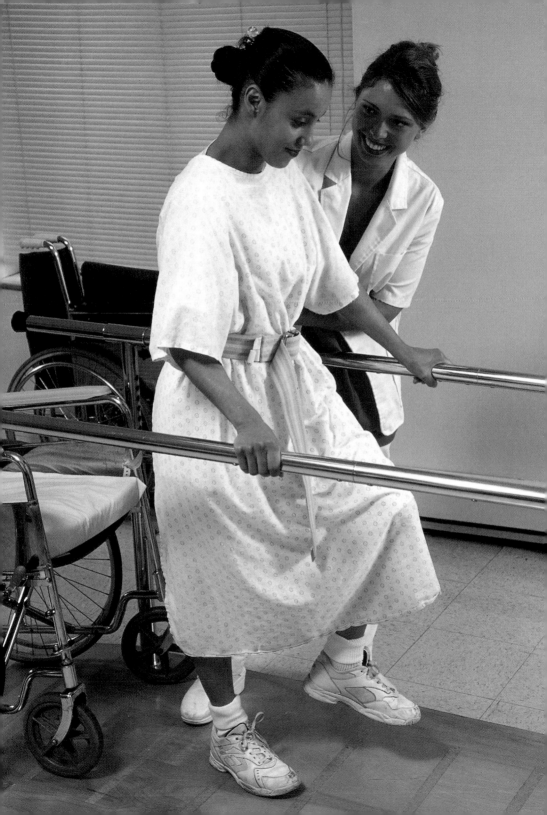

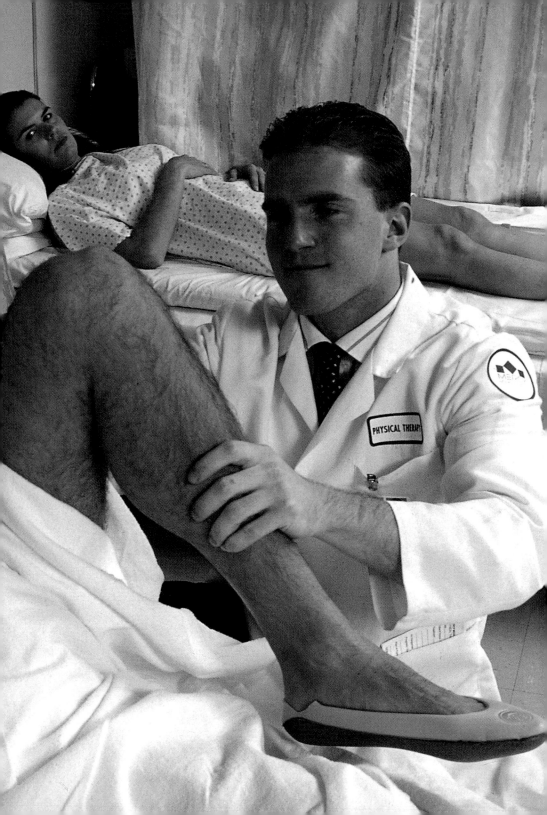

Chapter 2

What the Job Is Like

Physical therapist assistants help physical therapists establish patients' needs. A stroke patient might need to learn how to use a fork and knife. An injured person might need to strengthen an arm or leg. Some patients must learn to use prostheses. A prosthesis is an artificial limb or body part. Artificial means made by people.

Physical therapist assistants help injured people strengthen arms and legs.

Physical therapist assistants help patients set goals for improving their abilities. They help develop plans for reaching those goals.

Many physical therapist assistants teach patients to perform daily living skills in new ways. They teach patients to feed and groom themselves. They teach patients to use wheelchairs, crutches, and prostheses. These new ways of living help patients cope with the changes in their bodies.

Helping Patients Exercise

Physical therapist assistants help patients improve their health through exercise. Patients can strengthen their muscles through exercise. Physical therapist assistants help patients use weight machines, parallel bars, and other equipment.

Physical therapist assistants also help patients through passive exercise. Passive exercise is when a physical therapist assistant moves and

Physical therapist assistants help patients improve their health through exercise.

stretches a patient's limbs. Passive exercise helps patients move better on their own.

Exercise can help patients regain their physical abilities. It can also prevent injuries from becoming worse. Physical therapist assistants watch patients during both active and passive exercise. They take notes about patients' progress. Then they report this information to physical therapists.

Other Treatments

Physical therapist assistants use other treatments to reduce patients' pain. They use massage to relax sore muscles. Physical therapist assistants use whirlpool baths to relieve patients' sore muscles. They use ice to reduce swelling from injuries.

Physical therapist assistants use heat to relax muscles and make patients more comfortable. They use heating pads and lamps to apply heat. They also use ultrasound treatments to heal

Physical therapist assistants use whirlpool baths to relieve patients' sore muscles.

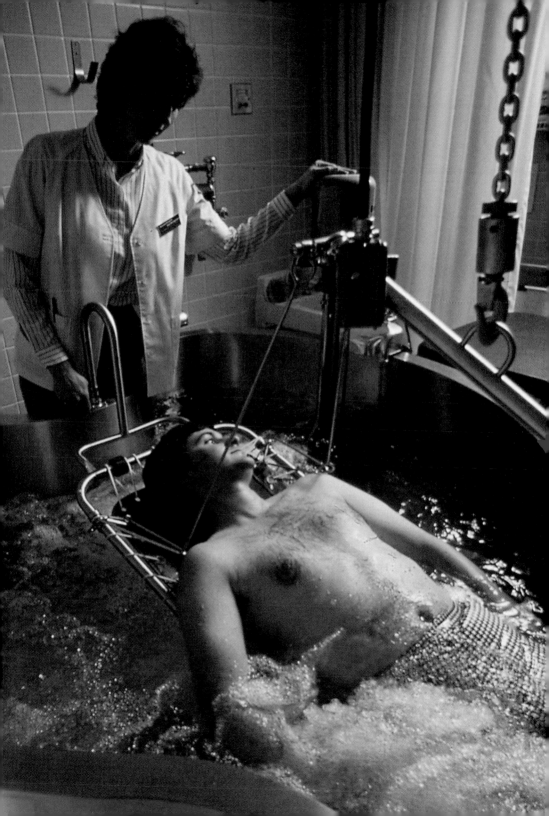

patients' body parts. Ultrasound is sound that is too high for humans to hear. These sound waves help heal the body.

Other Duties

Physical therapist assistants must be concerned about patients' emotions. Patients who become discouraged may advance more slowly. Physical therapist assistants support and encourage patients throughout treatment. Physical therapist assistants tell patients that they are making progress. They show patients how well they are doing.

Some physical therapist assistants work with patients' families. They teach family members how to perform passive exercises. They also show families how important it is to encourage patients.

Many physical therapist assistants perform office duties. They order supplies, organize files, and answer phones. They schedule appointments and keep records.

Physical therapist assistants support and encourage patients during treatment.

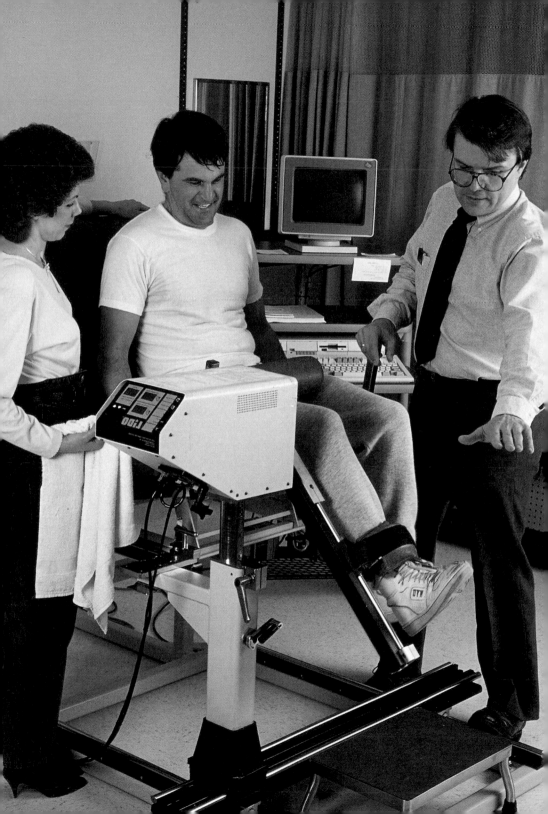

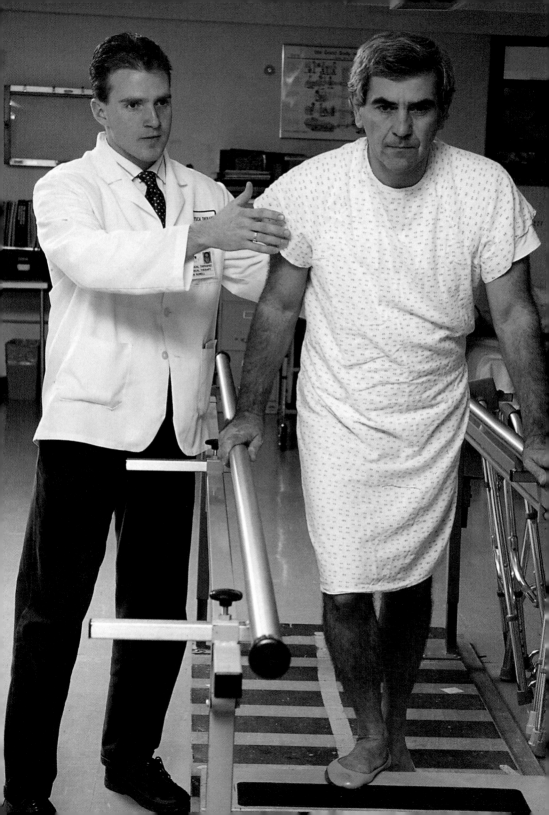

Personal Characteristics

Physical therapy is a demanding field. Physical therapist assistants must be physically strong. They must be able to bend and lift. They must be able to move patients and help them exercise. People who want to become physical therapist assistants should be physically fit.

Physical therapist assistants must be calm. They must help patients do the same exercises over and over. Some patients do not show progress for a long time. Physical therapist assistants must be persistent and upbeat. Persistent means to keep trying. They must be able to encourage patients who are discouraged. Physical therapist assistants must enjoy working with people. Caring about patients is the most important part of being a physical therapist assistant.

Physical therapist assistants are always supervised by physical therapists. They must be able to follow directions carefully. They must pay

Physical therapist assistants must be able to help patients exercise.

attention to detail and keep accurate records. They must be able to speak and write well. They also must clearly report information to physical therapists.

Work Settings

Physical therapist assistants often work in hospitals. They also work in rehabilitation centers and long-term care facilities. Rehabilitation centers are places where patients and therapists work to overcome disabilities. Long-term care facilities are places where patients can live and heal for long time periods.

Many physical therapist assistants work in nursing homes or for government health agencies. An agency is an office that provides a service to the public. Some physical therapist assistants work in schools for people with disabilities. Others work in private practices. This means that they work in offices or clinics owned by physical therapists.

Physical therapist assistants often work in hospitals and rehabilitation centers.

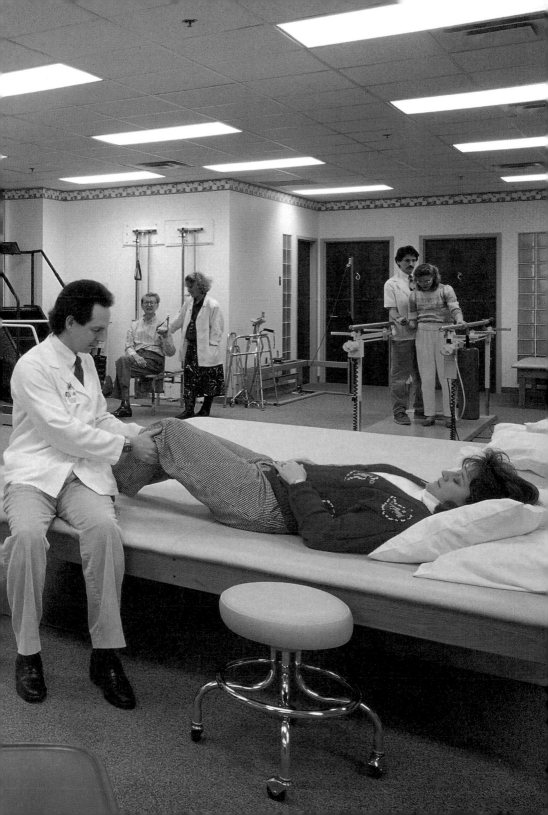

Chapter 3

Training

Physical therapist assistants must graduate from an accredited two-year program. Accredited programs have been approved by a recognized authority. Many community and junior colleges offer accredited physical therapist assistant programs.

In the United States and Canada, the Commission on Accreditation in Physical Therapy Education must approve programs. The American Physical Therapy Association and the Canadian Physiotherapy Association support the commission.

Many community and junior colleges offer accredited physical therapist assistant programs.

Two-year programs

Most physical therapist assistant programs last two years. These programs combine classes with clinical experience. Students earn an associate's degree when they graduate from these programs.

Students take classes in anatomy and physiology. Anatomy is the study of the human body. Physiology is the study of how the body works. Students learn about bones, muscles, and joints. They also learn about human growth and development.

Students in physical therapist assistant programs learn basic teaching skills. They must be able to teach patients to use equipment and to perform exercises. Students also study different kinds of massage, exercise treatments, and heat and cold therapy.

Students train in clinics or hospitals after they have completed some classes. Physical therapists closely supervise students during students' clinical practice. This training experience helps students understand the responsibilities of being a physical therapist assistant.

Physical therapist assistants schedule appointments and keep records.

License Requirements

Most states require physical therapist assistants to have special licenses. Assistants must graduate from accredited programs to get licenses. Most states also require physical therapist assistants to pass a written test. Each state has different requirements. Students should contact state licensing boards for more information.

Many workplaces require physical therapist assistants to have certification in cardiopulmonary resuscitation (CPR). Certification is official recognition of a person's abilities or skills. CPR is a method of restarting a heart that has stopped beating. CPR involves breathing into a patient's mouth. It also involves pressing on a patient's chest in a certain rhythm.

Exploring This Career

Students interested in becoming physical therapist assistants can start preparing now. There are many helpful classes. Health, biology, and anatomy classes help students understand how bodies work. Computer courses are also important. Physical therapist assistants use computers to schedule appointments and keep records.

Physical therapist assistants need good language skills. English and speech classes can increase language skills. Good language skills help physical therapist assistants explain procedures to patients.

Instructors closely supervise students during their clinical practice.

Students can gain valuable experience by volunteering. Volunteer means to offer to do a job without pay. Some people volunteer at physical therapy departments. Others volunteer to assist students with disabilities in schools. Working at a summer camp for children with disabilities is also good experience.

Finding Jobs

Students can find jobs through their schools' guidance offices. They can find positions by reading employment sections of newspapers. Employment agencies can also help people find jobs.

Employers look for assistants who have graduated from accredited physical therapist assistant programs. They prefer physical therapist assistants who have experience. Beginning assistants who have volunteer experience in physical therapy will have an advantage.

Employers prefer physical therapist assistants who have experience.

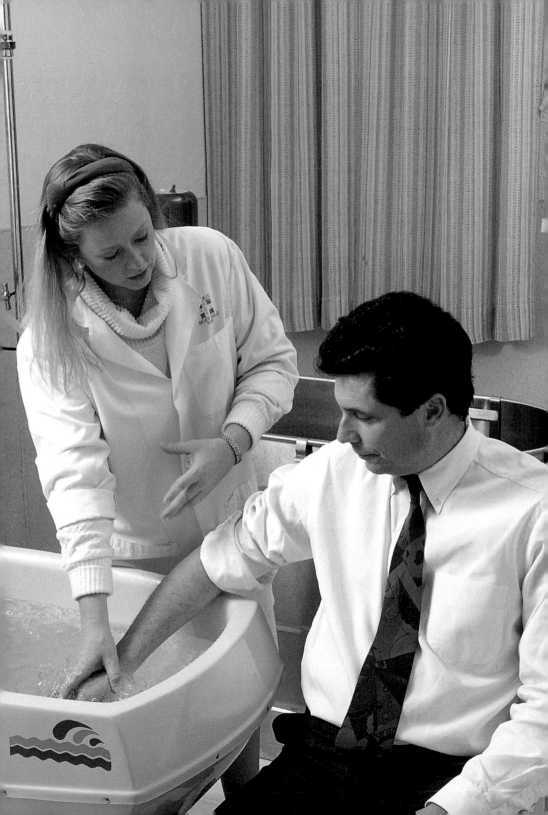

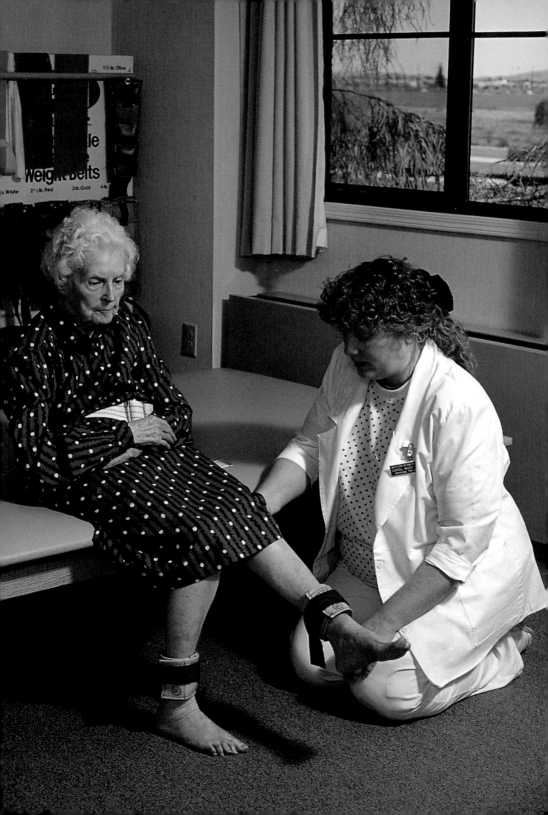

Chapter 4

Salary and Job Outlook

Beginning physical therapist assistants may earn between $20,000 and $23,000 per year. Experienced assistants may earn between $25,000 and $48,000. Assistants who work in private practices usually earn the highest salaries.

Most physical therapist assistants receive benefits. Benefits are payments or services provided by employers in addition to a salary or wages. Benefits may include health insurance,

Physical therapist assistants who work in private practice usually earn the highest salaries.

Physical therapy helps people recover from sports injuries.

paid vacations, paid holidays, and pensions. Health insurance is protection from the costs of getting sick. People pay small amounts to insurance companies each month. The insurance companies pay most of the bills if people become sick. A pension is payments made to older people who have retired.

Job Outlook

Physical therapy is a rapidly growing field. Experts believe this field will continue to expand for many years. There are several reasons for this growth.

First, many people in North America are older than 65 years old. Older people need physical therapy more often than younger people. Physical therapy can help older people who have arthritis or injuries. It also helps them recover from strokes and other illnesses.

Second, recent laws require better services for people with disabilities. Physical therapy helps people with disabilities gain mobility. Mobility is the ability to move. It helps them strengthen weak muscles and remain healthy.

Third, many people exercise regularly. People can get injured during sports or exercise. Physical therapy helps people recover from these injuries.

Employers are hiring more physical therapist assistants because there are not enough physical therapists. Assistants can carry out rehabilitation plans developed by physical therapists. Then the physical therapists can see more patients.

Chapter 5

Where the Job Can Lead

Physical therapist assistants can advance in many ways. Assistants may perform complex treatments after they gain experience. Others may help run physical therapy departments. Those who work in large departments sometimes supervise other assistants. Supervisors assign duties and plan schedules for other assistants.

Experienced physical therapist assistants may perform complex treatments.

Specialists

Physical therapist assistants may decide to specialize in a single area. Specialize means to focus on one area of work.

Some specialists work only with elderly patients. Others may work with people who have had strokes. Some specialists like to work with children.

Sports Medicine

A growing field for physical therapist assistants is sports medicine. These assistants are experts at helping people who have been injured while playing sports. Assistants in this field often work for professional sports teams.

Athletes often suffer from injuries that are different from other peoples' injuries. Physical therapist assistants understand these special needs. They know how to use various therapies to help athletes recover from injuries.

Physical therapist assistants use various therapies to help athletes recover from injuries.

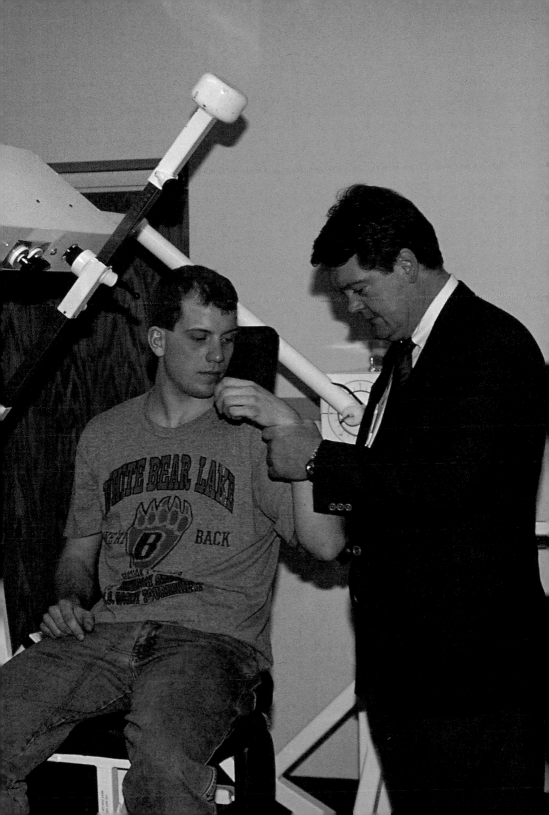

Additional Training

Some physical therapist assistants decide to become physical therapists. These individuals return to school to earn master's degrees. A master's degree requires a four-year college degree plus two more years of training. Most students find that their experience as physical therapist assistants is valuable. They like helping people relieve pain. They want to learn even more about helping patients.

Most physical therapist assistants find their experiences very valuable.

Words to Know

amputate (AM-pyuh-tate)—to remove a limb

anatomy (uh-NAT-uh-mee)—the study of the human body

arthritis (ar-THRYE-tiss)—a disease that affects joints

cardiopulmonary resuscitation (CPR) (kar-dee-oh-PUHL-muh-nair-ee ree-se-se-TAY-shuhn)—a method of restarting a heart that has stopped beating; it involves breathing into a patient's mouth and pressing on a patient's chest in a certain rhythm

certification (sur-tif-uh-KAY-shun)—official recognition of a person's abilities or skills

massage (muh-SAHZH)—the steady pressing and moving of muscles

physical therapy (FIZ-uh-kuhl THER-uh-pee)—the treatment of diseased or hurt muscles and joints using exercise, massage, and heat

prosthesis (pross-THEE-siss)—an artificial limb or body part

specialize (SPESH-uh-lize)—to focus on one area of work

stroke (STROHK)—when a blood vessel breaks in the brain

ultrasound (UHL-truh-sound)—sound that is too high for humans to hear; the sound waves help heal the body

volunteer (vol-uhn-TIHR)—to offer to do a job without pay

To Learn More

Careers in Physical Therapy: Physical Therapist, Physical Therapy Assistant. Chicago: Institute for Research, 1996.

James, Robert. *Physical Therapists*. Vero Beach, Fla.: Rourke Book Co., 1995.

Krumhansl, Bernice. *Opportunities in Physical Therapy Careers*. Lincolnwood, Ill.: VGM Career Horizons, 1993.

Wilkinson, Beth. *Careers Inside the World of Health Care*. New York: Rosen Publishing Group, 1995.

Useful Addresses

American Physical Therapy Association
1111 North Fairfax Street
Alexandria, VA 22314

Canadian Physiotherapy Association
2345 Yonge Street
Suite 410
Toronto, ON M4P 2E5
Canada

New York Physical Therapy Association
4 Palisades Drive
Suite 220
Executive Woods
Albany, NY 12205

Internet Sites

American Physical Therapy Association
http://www.apta.org

Canadian Physiotherapy Association
http://www.physiotherapy.ca

New York Physical Therapy Association
http://www.nypta.org/

Physical Therapy Assistants and Aides
http://stats.bls.gov/oco/ocos167.htm

Index